LANDMARK TOP TENS

The World's Most Amazing
Castles

Ann Weil

www.raintreepublishers.co.uk
Visit our website to find out more information about Raintree books.

To order:
☎ Phone 0845 6044371
📄 Fax +44 (0) 1865 312263
📧 Email myorders@raintreepublishers.co.uk

Customers from outside the UK please telephone +44 1865 312262

Raintree is an imprint of **Capstone Global Library Limited**, a company incorporated in England and Wales having its registered office at 7 Pilgrim Street, London, EC4V 6LB – Registered company number: 6695582

Text © Capstone Global Library Limited 2012
First published in hardback in 2012
The moral rights of the proprietor have been asserted.

Edited by Megan Cotugno and Laura Knowles
Designed by Victoria Allen
Original illustrations © Capstone Global Library Ltd (2011)
Illustrated by Oxford Designers and Illustrators and HL Studios
Picture research by Hannah Taylor and Ruth Blair
Production by Camilla Crask
Originated by Capstone Global Library Ltd
Printed in China by CTPS

ISBN 978 1 4062 2750 5 (hardback)
15 14 13 12 11
10 9 8 7 6 5 4 3 2 1

British Library Cataloguing in Publication Data
Weil, Ann.
   The world's most amazing castles. -- (Landmark top tens)
   1. Castles--Juvenile literature.
   I. Title II. Series
   728.8'1-dc22
A full catalogue record for this book is available from the British Library.

Acknowledgements
We would like to thank the following for permission to reproduce photographs: Alamy Images pp. 6 (© Sindre Ellingsen), 9 (© Dieter Wanke), 12 (© Stephen Saks Photography), 20 (© Alex Segre), 21 (© Porky Pies Photography), 23 (© Peter Titmuss), 26 and 27 (© dbimages); Corbis p. 15 (Asian Art & Archaeology, Inc); Photolibrary pp. 8 (First Light Associated Photographers/Miles Ertman), 10 (P. Narayan), 13 (imagebroker/Jevgenija Pigozne), 17 (Fridmar Damm), 22 (Hoberman Collection UK); Rex Features pp. 11 (Sipa Press), 18; Shutterstock pp. 5 (© St Nick), 14 (© Martin Mette), 16 (© Worakit Sirijinda), 19 (© salajean), 24 (© Maugli), 25 (© Konstantin Mironov).

Cover photograph of Schloss Neuschwanstein near Fussen, Bavaria (Bayern), Germany, reproduced with permission of Photolibrary (Robert Harding).

We would like to thank Daniel Block for his invaluable help in the preparation of this book.

Every effort has been made to contact copyright holders of material reproduced in this book. Any omissions will be rectified in subsequent printings if notice is given to the publisher.

Contents

Some words are printed in bold, **like this**. You can find out what they mean in the glossary.

Castles

Nobles began building castles in Europe in the 800s and 900s CE. Many of the first castles were like forts. Wealthy people needed protection from robbers and enemy attacks. Wooden towers, called keeps, were constructed on steep hills. This made it easier to see danger from far away. It was also more difficult for enemies to attack when they were going uphill.

Some castles had deep ditches called moats around the outside. Sometimes moats were filled with water. Sometimes they were dry. The people who lived in the castle used a **drawbridge** to cross the moat.

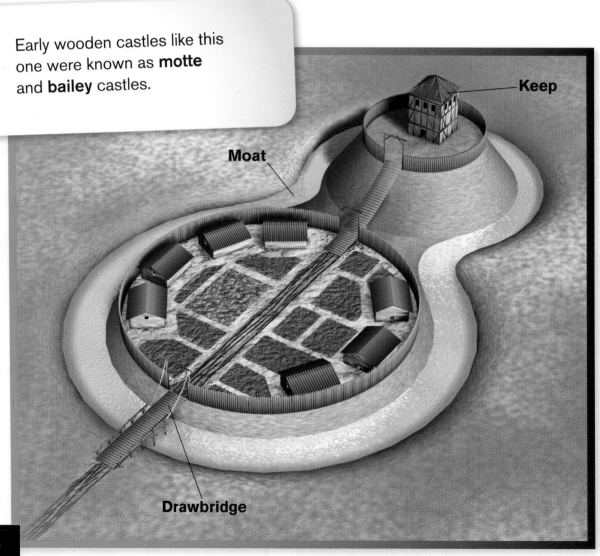

Early wooden castles like this one were known as **motte** and **bailey** castles.

Keep

Moat

Drawbridge

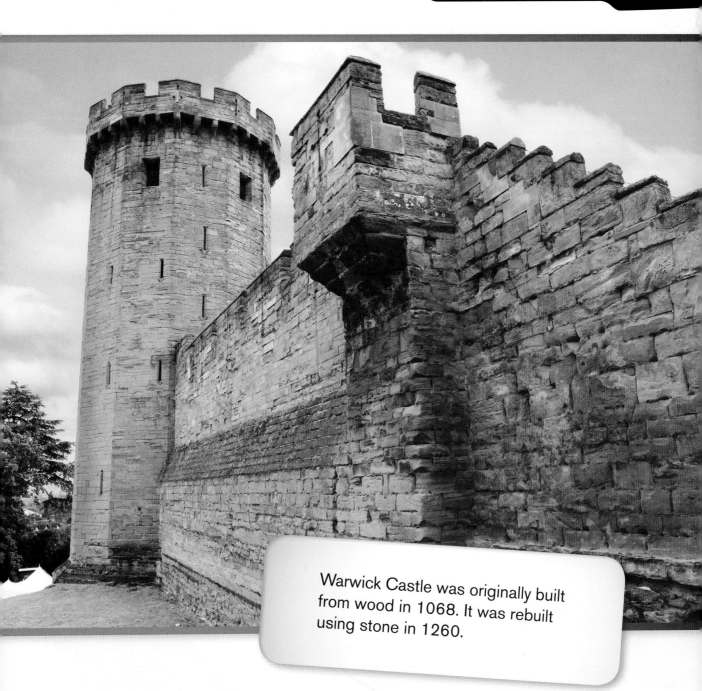

Warwick Castle was originally built from wood in 1068. It was rebuilt using stone in 1260.

Wood versus stone

Wooden castles were easy and quick to build. But wood burns, so wooden castles could easily go up in flames. Later, castles were made from stone with high walls and towers. Some castles had both inner and outer walls to make it even more difficult for enemies to get all the way inside.

Krak des Chevaliers

Krak des Chevaliers means "fortress of the knights". This castle in Syria has stone walls that are almost 3 metres (10 feet) thick. It was built to be able to withstand a **siege** of up to five years. The knights stored extra food inside, just in case. There was also a **well** within the castle so that enemies could not cut off the water supply.

Krak des Chevaliers

Location: Syria, the Middle East

Size: 3,000 square metres (32,291 square feet)

That's amazing!
This castle looks as it did a thousand years ago, when real knights walked through its halls.

Krak des Chevaliers was never attacked, and remains intact to this day.

Krak des Chevaliers was built during the 10th century at a time of religious wars, called the Crusades. **Christian** European **nobles** sent knights and soldiers to the **Middle East**. There they fought against **Muslim** Turks for control of the Holy Land, especially the city of Jerusalem. Many castles were built during this era. They guarded important roads in the lands where the Crusades were fought.

Krak des Chevaliers is probaly the most famous of the many castles that were built in the Middle East by the Christian knights during the Crusades.

Malbork Castle

The building of Malbork Castle in Poland started in around 1276. This castle was also the home for a group of Crusaders. After the Crusades, these knights ruled the countryside around them for more than 150 years.

Malbork Castle was listed as a **World Heritage Site** in 1997. Only very special places are given this honour.

Malbork Castle

Location: Malbork, Poland

Size: 143,591 square metres (1,545,600 square feet)

That's amazing!
It's one of the largest castles in the world!

A Gothic castle

Malbork is the largest brick Gothic castle in Europe. Gothic refers to a style of **architecture**. Gothic castles have high, curved ceilings. The arches are pointed instead of round. The high walls could fall down if it weren't for **flying buttresses**, which stick out from the wall and help support the roof.

Time to go!

The knights of Malbork had an unusual way of killing their enemies. They pretended to invite them inside as guests. Then they threw them down the toilet! Medieval castle toilets were built over holes in the outer wall that emptied into a moat.

Arg-é Bam Castle

Arg-é Bam was built around 500 BCE. At that time it was the most impressive building in the region then known as Persia. The **citadel** included food storage buildings, gardens, houses, and **wells**.

Arg-é Bam was surrounded by six-metre- (20-foot-) high **adobe** walls.

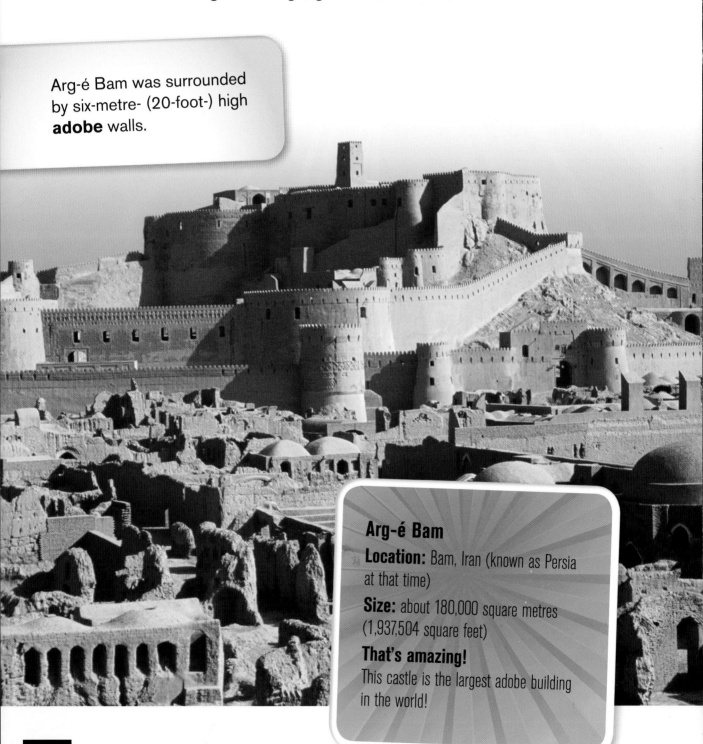

Arg-é Bam
Location: Bam, Iran (known as Persia at that time)

Size: about 180,000 square metres (1,937,504 square feet)

That's amazing!
This castle is the largest adobe building in the world!

The Silk Road

Arg-é Bam was an important stop along the **Silk Road**. This was not a single road, but many trade routes that connected China and Europe. It cut through the deserts of Central Asia. Traders carrying silk, spices, and other goods travelled together in large groups, called caravans. They hoped this would keep them safe from robbers. Camels were the only animals hardy enough to carry goods along this treacherous route.

In 2003 an earthquake almost completely destroyed Arg-é Bam. Other nations are helping the government of Iran rebuild this amazing castle.

Predjamski Grad

Predjamski Grad means "castle built in front of a cave". The first castle was probably built in Slovenia in the 1100s. It became known as a hideout for robbers and bandits. In the 1400s a knight called Erazem lived in the castle. One of his **ancestors** had built the original castle.

This is one of the three ways into the cave under the castle.

Predjamski Grad

Location: Slovenia, central Europe

Size: About 570 metres (1,870 feet) in length and an average of 130 metres (427 feet) wide

That's amazing!
This amazing castle is built into the side of a cliff!

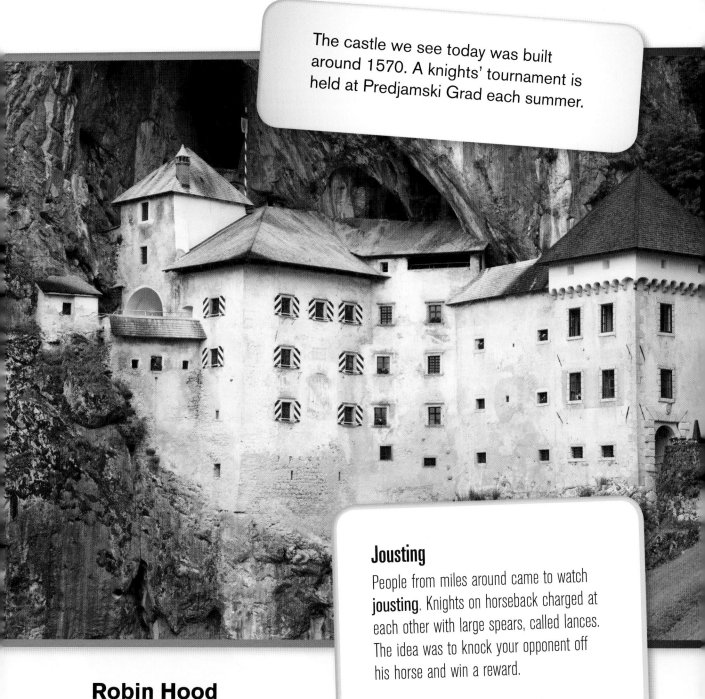

The castle we see today was built around 1570. A knights' tournament is held at Predjamski Grad each summer.

Jousting

People from miles around came to watch **jousting**. Knights on horseback charged at each other with large spears, called lances. The idea was to knock your opponent off his horse and win a reward.

Robin Hood

Erazem became known as a local Robin Hood. He and his men used secret tunnels from the caves to smuggle in food when they were under **siege**. Stories say he was betrayed and murdered inside the castle.

Himeji Castle

Himeji Castle in Japan is known as the White **Heron** Castle. Construction of this elegant castle began in the 1330s. It was enlarged many times over the next 300 years. The castle is on top of a steep hill, surrounded by three moats. Its walls are almost 15 metres (50 feet) high. However, Himeji Castle was never attacked.

Himeji Castle

Location: Himeji, Japan

Size: 230,000 square metres (2,,475,000 square feet)

That's amazing!
This castle is said to be haunted by the ghost of a servant girl!

Himeji is the best-preserved castle in Japan.

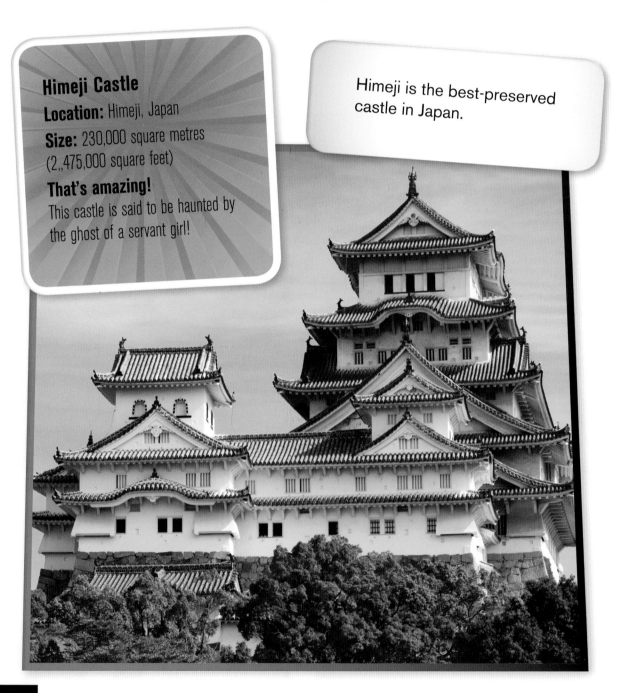

The ghost of Himeji Castle

There are rumours that the ghost of a servant girl haunts Himeji Castle. In one version of the story, a maid called Okiku broke one of 10 valuable plates. In a rage, the lord of the castle killed her and threw her down the castle **well**. Every night her ghost comes out of the well. She counts from one to nine, and then bursts out crying.

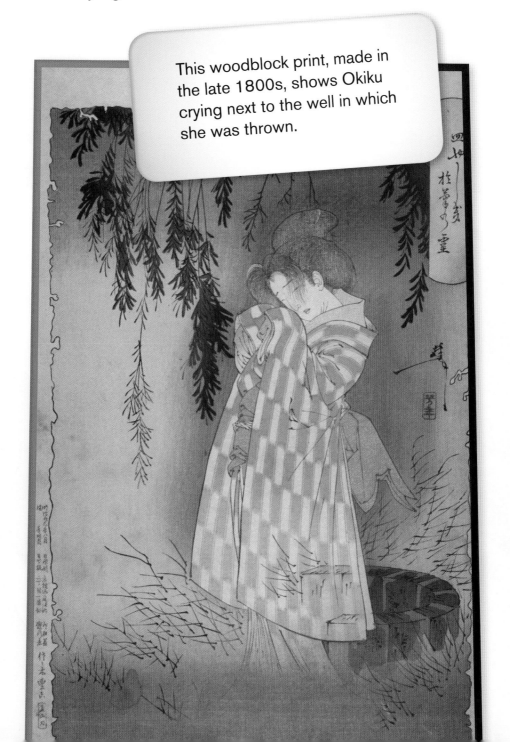

This woodblock print, made in the late 1800s, shows Okiku crying next to the well in which she was thrown.

Windsor Castle

Around 1070 King William I (the Conqueror) built a wooden fort in Windsor. It was meant to defend the road to London. Over the years other kings and queens added on new stone buildings. King John fought off two **sieges** from Windsor Castle. Queen Elizabeth I went there to escape the **plague** in London.

What began as a simple wooden fort is now a magnificent stone fortress.

Windsor Castle

Location: United Kingdom

Size: Floor area is 52,609 square metres (566,280 square feet)

That's amazing!
It's the largest **inhabited** castle in the world.

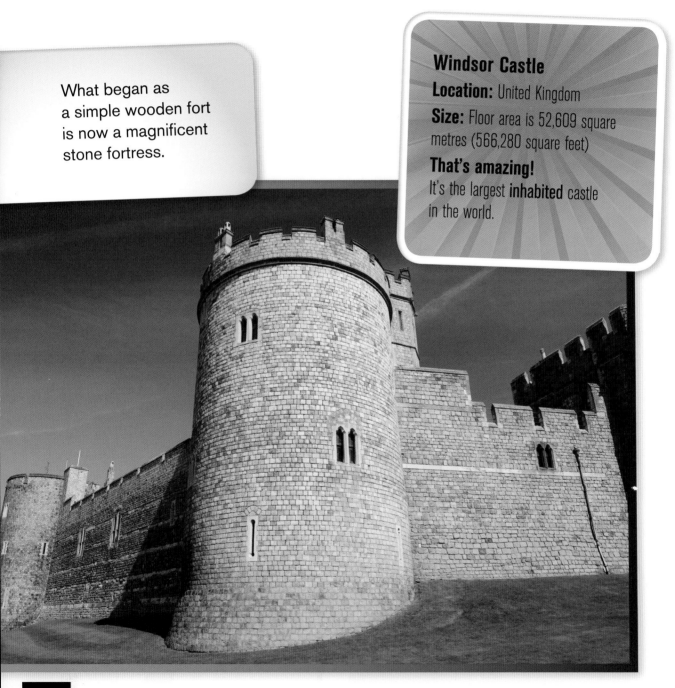

There are about 1,000 rooms in Windsor Castle.

Windsor Castle fire

In 1992 the castle was badly damaged by a fire. It started in the Queen's Private Chapel, when a spotlight set a curtain on fire. The flames were finally put out more than 12 hours later.

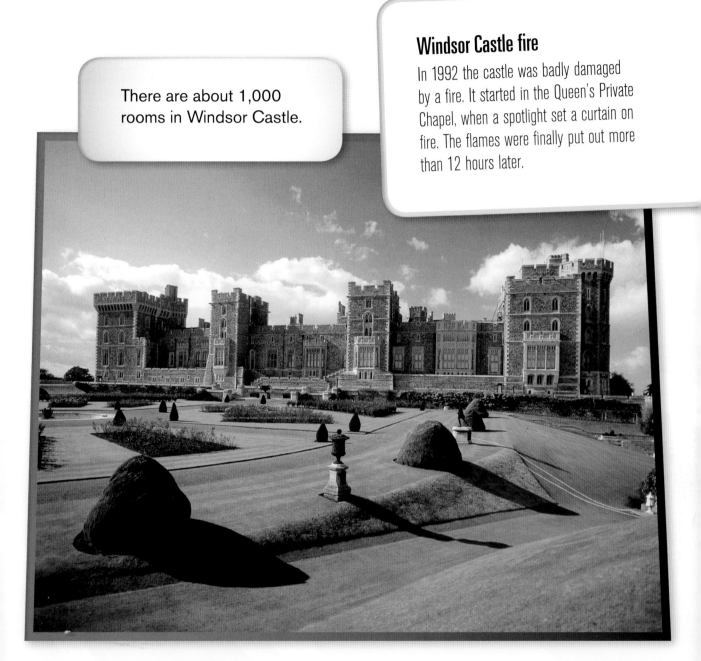

Windsor Castle today

For more than 900 years Windsor Castle has been a home for British royalty. That's a world record for any castle! Today, it is one of the official homes of Queen Elizabeth II.

Castles of horror!

Count Dracula and Dr. Victor Frankenstein are fictional characters in novels. But they may have been based on real people and places.

Castle Frankenstein

Did Mary Shelley set her famous novel *Frankenstein*, in the real-life Castle Frankenstein in Germany? It's possible that Shelley might have seen the castle and heard stories of an **alchemist** who lived there in the 1700s. Whether or not it inspired her to write the story, this castle has become associated with her horror novel. Now, it hosts a show full of monsters every Halloween.

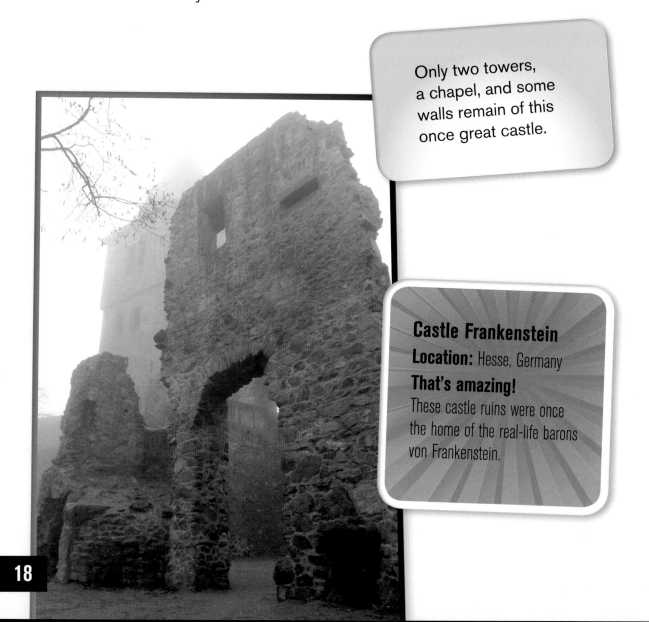

Only two towers, a chapel, and some walls remain of this once great castle.

Castle Frankenstein
Location: Hesse, Germany
That's amazing!
These castle ruins were once the home of the real-life barons von Frankenstein.

Dracula's castles?

Romanian prince Vlad the Impaler was the real-life model for Count Dracula. He was famous for torturing thousands of his enemies. Today, many castles in Romania are called "Dracula's Castle". Vlad the Impaler did not own them, but he may have been a prisoner at Hunyad Castle and Bran Castle in Romania.

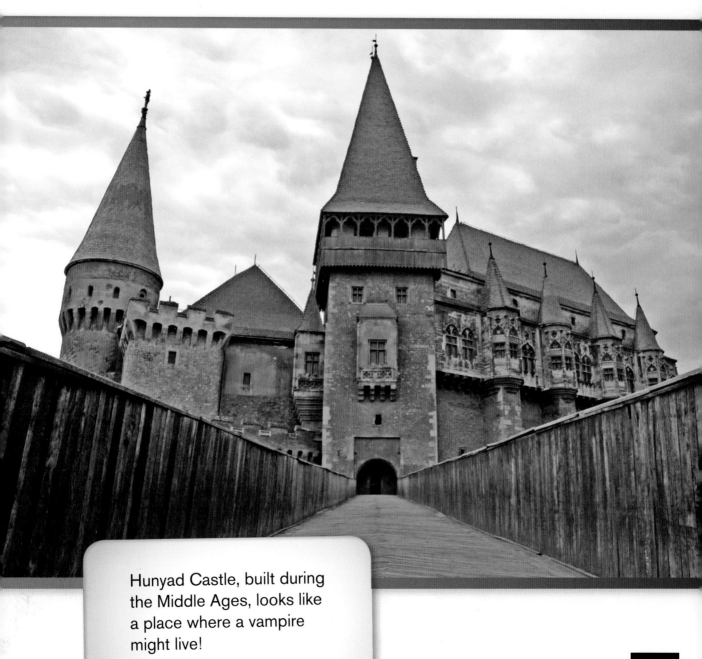

Hunyad Castle, built during the Middle Ages, looks like a place where a vampire might live!

Castillo de San Felipe de Barajas

Castillo de San Felipe de Barajas is in the port city of Cartagena in Colombia, South America. It defended the city from pirates – and the English! It began as a small fort on a hilltop. Then in the 16th century the Spanish government that controlled Colombia used slave labour to enlarge it. When it was finished, the fort covered the entire hill. It cost almost 227 tonnes of gold to build!

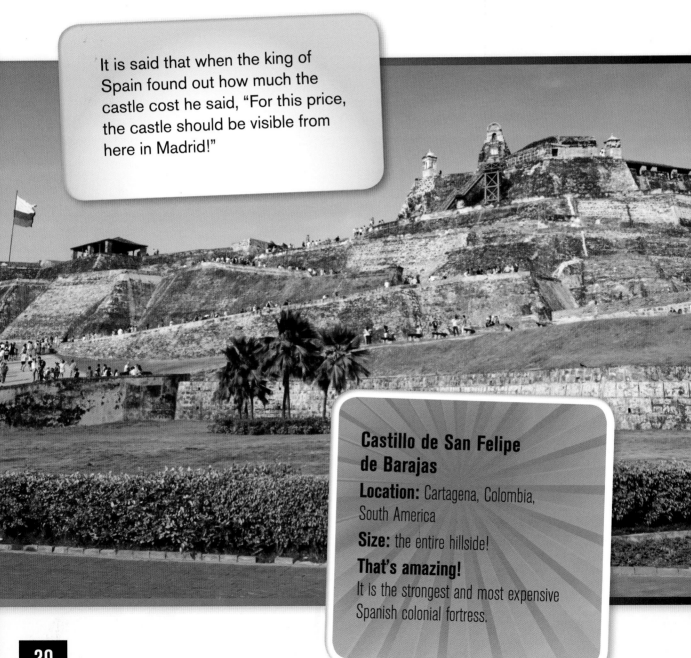

It is said that when the king of Spain found out how much the castle cost he said, "For this price, the castle should be visible from here in Madrid!"

Castillo de San Felipe de Barajas

Location: Cartagena, Colombia, South America

Size: the entire hillside!

That's amazing!
It is the strongest and most expensive Spanish colonial fortress.

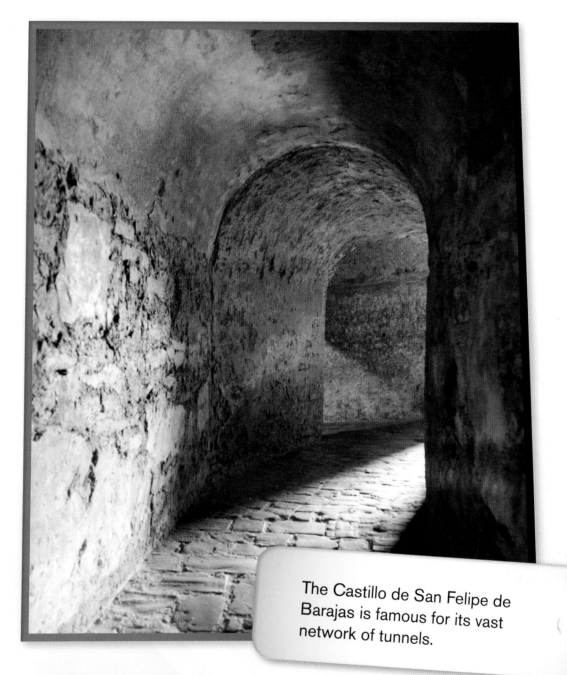

The Castillo de San Felipe de Barajas is famous for its vast network of tunnels.

Talking in tunnels

Underneath the castle there are miles of tunnels. These were used to bring in food during a **siege**. The tunnels were also carefully designed so that sound waves would carry well. This way, spoken messages could travel long distances. In a time long before mobile phones, this was a good way to communicate in the long, dark passageways.

Castle of Good Hope

The Dutch built this fort in the 1600s. At that time the Dutch ruled the southern tip of Africa, as well as island **colonies** in Southeast Asia. They needed a safe harbour in Africa so their ships could stop to take on more food and water for long voyages. They also needed a secure fort to protect themselves and their riches from pirates.

Castle of Good Hope
Location: Cape Town, South Africa
That's amazing!
The Castle of Good Hope is the oldest surviving building in South Africa.

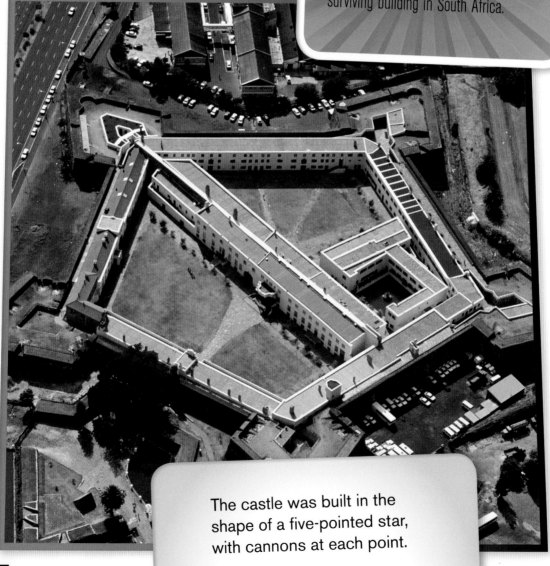

The castle was built in the shape of a five-pointed star, with cannons at each point.

Pirates!

The Castle of Good Hope was originally built on the beach overlooking the sea. But over time the sea washed up enough rock and sand to form an area of land between the castle and the sea shore. The castle is now two kilometres inland!

The Castle of Good Hope was made a national monument in 1936. Today, it is used for military ceremonies and as a military museum.

Neuschwanstein Castle

Neuschwanstein Castle was built for King Ludwig II of Bavaria in the late 1800s. He did not need it for protection. By that time, new castles were designed more like palaces than fortresses.

Neuschwanstein Castle

Location: Bavaria, Germany

Size: About 6,000 square metres (64,583 square feet) floor space

That's amazing!
It is the most photographed castle in the world!

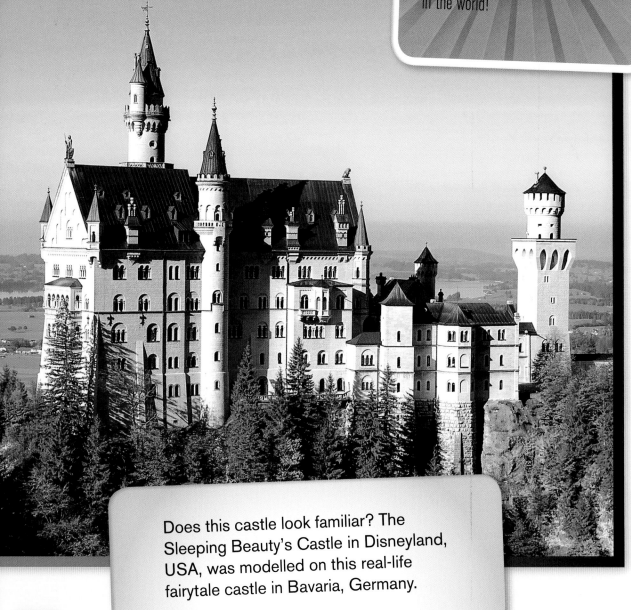

Does this castle look familiar? The Sleeping Beauty's Castle in Disneyland, USA, was modelled on this real-life fairytale castle in Bavaria, Germany.

The rooms inside the castle are interesting shapes with beautiful furniture and decorations.

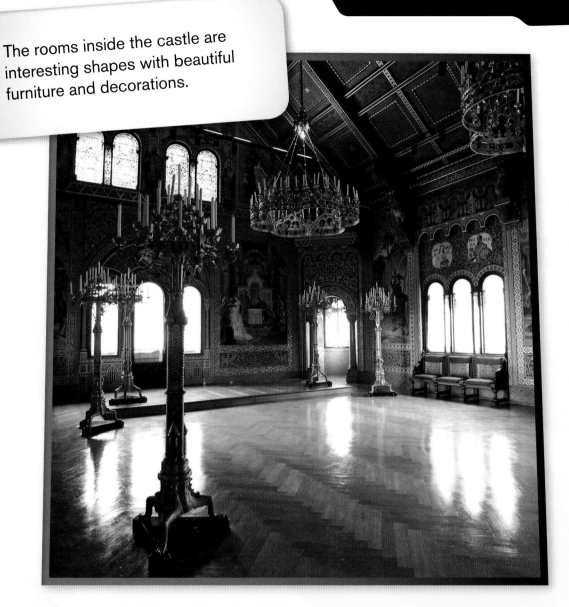

Mad King Ludwig

King Ludwig II did not live to see his masterpiece completed. In 1886, his government declared him insane (mad) and removed him from the throne. Then, with his castle almost finished, Ludwig was found dead. Was he murdered? Did he kill himself? His death remains a mystery.

Neuschwanstein Castle was opened to the public after the death of "Mad King Ludwig". It has been one of the most popular tourist attractions in Germany ever since. More than 50 million people have visited it!

Castles in danger

Like many old buildings, castles wear away over time. Castles in deserts are **eroded** by sandstorms. Castles in cities are damaged by air pollution. Natural disasters can also put castles in danger. For example, in 2003 an earthquake destroyed Arg-é Bam in Iran.

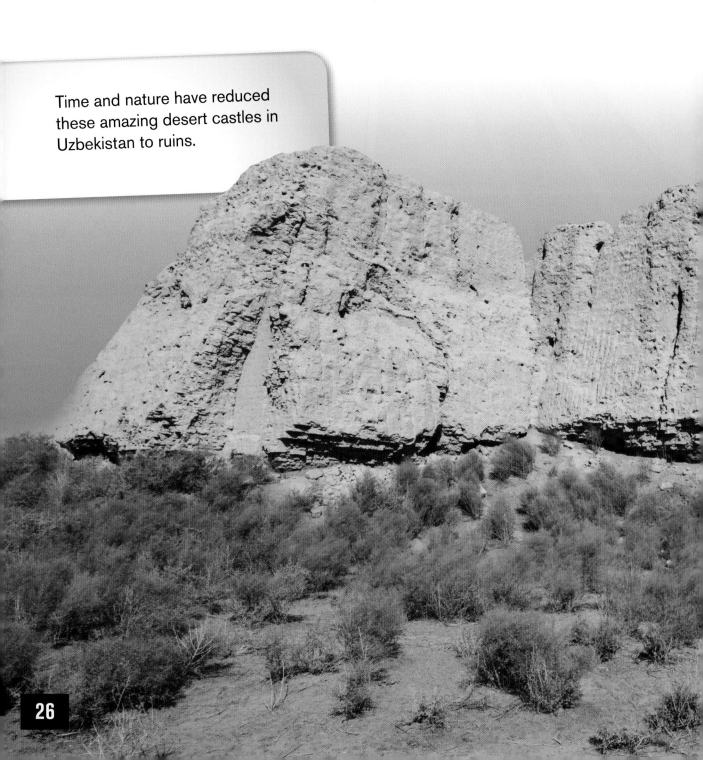

Time and nature have reduced these amazing desert castles in Uzbekistan to ruins.

Castles today

Some castles are now homes for the very rich, but most are no longer lived in. People do not need castles to defend them against enemy attacks. Even if they did, old castles, such as Krak des Chevaliers, could not withstand modern weapons. Many castles survive today because tourists pay to see them. The money is used for repairs and upkeep, so that people can continue to enjoy these amazing historical buildings.

Castle facts and figures

Most castles were built in Europe, but some can be found in Africa, Asia, and the Americas. The first castles were simple wooden forts, built for protection. Some castles are huge stone structures still standing today. Others are in ruins, destroyed during ancient or modern wars. Which castle do you think is the most amazing?

Krak des Chevaliers
Location: Syria, the Middle East
Size: 3,000 square metres (32,291 square feet)
That's amazing!
This castle looks as it did a thousand years ago, when real knights walked through its halls.

Malbork Castle
Location: Malbork, Poland
Size: 143,591 square metres (1,545,600 square feet)
That's amazing!
It's one of the largest castles in the world!

Arg-é Bam
Location: Bam, Iran (known as Persia at that time)
Size: about 180,000 square metres (1,937,504 square feet)
That's amazing!
This castle is the largest adobe building in the world!

Predjamski Grad
Location: Slovenia
Size: About 570 metres (1,870 feet) in length and an average of 130 metres (427 feet) wide
That's amazing!
This amazing castle is built into the side of a cliff!

Himeji Castle

Location: Himeji, Japan

Size: 230,000 square metres (2,,475,000 square feet)

That's amazing!
This castle is said to be haunted by the ghost of a servant girl!

Windsor Castle

Location: United Kingdom

Size: Floor area is 52,609 square metres (566,280 square feet)

That's amazing!
It's the largest **inhabited** castle in the world.

Castle Frankenstein

Location: Hesse, Germany

That's amazing!
These castle ruins were once the home of real-life barons von Frankenstein.

Castillo de San Felipe de Barajas

Location: Cartagena, Colombia, South America

Size: the entire hillside!

That's amazing!
It is the strongest and most expensive Spanish colonial fortress.

Castle of Good Hope

Location: Cape Town, South Africa

That's amazing!
The Castle of Good Hope is the oldest surviving building in South Africa.

Neuschwanstein Castle

Location: Bavaria, Germany

Size: About 6,000 square metres (64,583 square feet) floor space

That's amazing!
It is the most photographed castle in the world!

Glossary

adobe made with sun-dried clay bricks

alchemist person who believed he or she could turn any metal into gold or silver

ancestor grandparents, great-grandparents, and other relatives who lived a long time ago

architecture design and construction of buildings

Christian person who follows the teachings of Jesus Christ

bailey castle's outer wall and courtyard which surrounded the wooden tower, or keep

citadel fortress in a city

colony place that people from another country have occupied and settled in

drawbridge bridge that can be lifted up at one end to stop people from crossing

eroded worn away

flying buttress arched support for a wall

heron wading bird with long legs and neck

inhabited lived in

jousting competition between knights on horseback using lances

Middle East large area that includes the present-day countries of Egypt, Israel, Syria, Turkey, Iran, Iraq, and others

motte large mound of earth upon which a castle was built

Muslim person who is a follower of Islam

noble important, wealthy person

plague very infectious, deadly disease

siege when enemies surround a place to force those inside to surrender

Silk Road ancient trade route from Europe to China

well deep hole dug or drilled to get water

World Heritage Site place with outstanding historical value

Find out more

Books

A Year in a Castle, Rachel Coombs (Millbrook Press, 2009)

Castle, Christopher Gravett (DK Eyewitness book, 2008)

Castles, Stephanie Turnbull (Usborne Books, 2007)

The Age of Castles (series), Struan Reid, Peter Dennis,
      Richard Dargie, and Peter Hicks (Wayland, 2007)

Websites

http://www.castles.org/index.htm
Discover more about some world-famous castles.

**http://www.historyonthenet.com/Medieval_Life/types_
of_castle.htm**
This website tells you about all the different types of castles.

**http://www.historyonthenet.com/Medieval_Life/attacking_
a_castle.htm**
Find out about how castles were attacked and defended
in Medieval times.

Index